Disclaimer

The information provided in "*Passport to Freedom: A Comprehensive Guide to Acquiring Additional Citizenships*" is for general informational purposes only. While every effort has been made to ensure the accuracy and completeness of the information contained herein, the author and publisher make no representations or warranties of any kind, express or implied, about the accuracy, reliability, suitability, or availability concerning the content, information, products, services, or related graphics contained in this book for any purpose. Therefore, any reliance on such information is strictly at your own risk.

The content of this book is not intended to be a substitute for professional legal, financial, or immigration advice. Always seek the advice of qualified professionals with any questions regarding citizenship, immigration laws, tax obligations, and investment opportunities. The author and publisher disclaim any liability for any loss or damage incurred due to the use of or reliance upon the information provided in this book.

Copyright

Passport to Freedom: A Comprehensive Guide to Acquiring Additional Citizenships

About the Author

Sally Pederson

Sally Pederson is an internationally renowned speaker, global citizen, and expert on international money mastery. Having lived in five countries and traveled to over 50, she has dedicated her life to investigating business opportunities, taxes, and lifestyle options around the globe. Sally's extensive experience includes acquiring multiple residencies and dual citizenships, legally reducing her taxes to low single digits, and owning companies and real estate in various countries.

With over a decade of hands-on experience, Sally has navigated the complexities of international finance, established multiple bank accounts and making strategic investments worldwide. Her expertise is theoretical and practical, enabling her to help other business owners and entrepreneurs achieve the freedom and flexibility of the Global Citizen Lifestyle. Sally's goal is to empower individuals to live unrestricted by the control of any single government.

In her previous book, **International Money Mastery: Avoid These Common Mistakes When Reducing Taxes to Zero or Single Digits, Protecting Assets, and Gaining International Freedom with Residencies and Citizenships**, Sally shared the strategies and tactics she perfected over years of personal and professional exploration. Her insights have not just informed but transformed lives by providing a blueprint for financial freedom and global mobility.

Now, in **Passport to Freedom: A Comprehensive Guide to Acquiring Additional Citizenships**, Sally extends her expertise to those seeking the benefits of Multiple Citizenships. Whether you're a business owner, speaker, author, coach, or entrepreneur, this guide offers the knowledge and tools to navigate the complexities of acquiring additional passports and embracing the Global Citizen Lifestyle.

Sally Pederson's dedication to helping others achieve international freedom and financial security makes her a trusted and invaluable resource for anyone looking to expand their horizons and secure a future without borders. Join Sally on this journey and unlock the world with **Passport to Freedom**.

Connect with Sally Pederson and Global Citizen Life:

Website: https://www.GlobalCitizenLife.org

Email: info@GlobalCitizenLife.org

Social Media:

Website – www.GlobalCitizenLife.org

LinkedIn – https://www.linkedin.com/in/sallypederson1

Company LinkedIn:

https://www.linkedin.com/company/global-citizen-life

International Money Mastery

This book is your ultimate guide to creating bullet-proof financial and personal wealth. This book will teach you how to legally reduce your taxes to zero or single digits, obtain Multiple Citizenships and residencies, and protect your assets - all without breaking the law.

With International Money Mastery, you can unlock the secrets to legally lowering your taxes to a fraction of what you pay now, becoming a citizen of multiple countries, and safeguarding your hard-earned assets - all without breaking the law.

With International Money Mastery, you can achieve financial freedom without committing any illegal act. You can succeed without breaking the law.

Buy it on Amazon or Smashwords.

Living Tax-Free – The Global Citizen Lifestyle

This book covers everything from understanding the basics of international taxation to selecting the best countries for a tax-free lifestyle. Learn about legal strategies, residency and citizenship programs, and how to set up your financial life abroad. Featuring real-life case studies and success stories, this guide provides valuable insights from those who have successfully navigated the path to tax-free living.

Buy it on Amazon or Smashwords.

Moving Abroad Journal – If Not Now, When?

Embark on your journey to a world of new horizons and endless possibilities with the "Global Citizen Life: Moving Abroad Journal." This meticulously designed journal is your essential companion for a seamless and inspiring transition to life abroad.

Are you ready to become a global citizen, diversify your life, and unlock the doors to a world of opportunities? Founder of Global Citizen Life, Sally Pederson, has crafted this journal with the expertise and passion to guide you through every step of your international adventure. Buy it on Amazon.

Introduction

Welcome to "**Passport to Freedom: A Comprehensive Guide to Acquiring Additional Passports.**" In an increasingly interconnected world, the ability to move freely across borders, access new economic opportunities, and safeguard your personal and financial well-being has never been more critical. This book is your essential guide to understanding the myriad pathways to securing second, third, or even fourth passports, unlocking the doors to global freedom.

Having Multiple Citizenships isn't just a luxury for the wealthy or the adventurous—it's a practical strategy for anyone looking to enhance their personal and professional lives. Multiple Citizenships can offer unparalleled mobility, security, and opportunity advantages. A second passport can provide a crucial safety net in an era marked by political instability, economic fluctuations, and frequent travel restrictions.

This book is designed for anyone interested in expanding their horizons and enhancing global mobility. Whether you're an entrepreneur looking to tap into new markets, a digital nomad seeking more travel flexibility, or a retiree planning for a secure and enriching future, this guide will provide you with the knowledge and tools to make informed decisions about acquiring additional passports.

Why This Book?

The journey to Multiple Citizenships can be complex, involving various legal, financial, and cultural considerations. "Passport to Freedom" aims to demystify this process by providing comprehensive information on the different pathways to acquiring additional passports. From citizenship by investment programs to naturalization and citizenship by descent, this book covers all the major routes and provides practical advice on each.

What You Will Learn

- **Understanding Dual and Multiple Citizenships**: Learn the basics, including the benefits and potential challenges of holding multiple citizenships.

- **The Legal Landscape**: Gain insights into international laws and treaties and country-specific regulations that affect dual and multiple citizenships.

- **Methods of Acquiring Additional Passports**: Explore various pathways such as citizenship by birth, descent, naturalization, marriage, investment, and special programs.

- **The Application Process**: Get step-by-step guidance on gathering necessary documents, filling out applications, preparing for interviews, and handling background checks.

- **Managing Multiple Passports**: Understand the legal obligations, practical considerations for travel, and strategies for cultural integration in your new country.

- **Case Studies and Success Stories**: Learn from real-life examples and expert insights to help guide your journey.

- **Resources and Further Reading**: Access a curated list of useful websites, organizations, books, and articles for additional information and support.

A Word from Global Citizen Life

At Global Citizen Life, we are dedicated to helping individuals achieve their dreams of global citizenship. Our mission is to provide you with the tools, resources, and support to navigate the complexities of acquiring and managing multiple citizenships. Whether you are an entrepreneur seeking new business opportunities, a retiree looking for a new place to call home, or simply someone who values global citizenship's freedom and flexibility, we are here to guide you every step of the way.

Embark on Your Journey

By embracing the challenge of change and innovation, you are not just obtaining additional passports—you are building a life that transcends borders and opens up a world of possibilities. We encourage you to take bold steps, explore new horizons, and create a future where you can thrive as a global citizen.

Thank you for joining us on this journey. We wish you the best of luck in pursuing Multiple Citizenships and a fulfilling global lifestyle. Welcome to Global Citizen Life—your passport to freedom and opportunity.

Let's get started!

Contents

**Passport to Freedom: A Comprehensive
Guide to Acquiring Additional Citizenships**

Welcome to Global Freedom

Welcome to "Passport to Freedom: A Comprehensive Guide
to Acquiring Additional Citizenships." In an increasingly
interconnected world, the ability to move freely across
borders, access new economic opportunities, and safeguard
your personal and financial well-being has never been more
critical. This book is your essential guide to understanding
the myriad pathways to securing second, third, or even fourth
passports, unlocking the doors to global freedom.

The Importance of Multiple Passports

Having multiple passports isn't just a luxury for the wealthy
or the adventurous—it's a practical strategy for anyone
looking to enhance their personal and professional lives.
Multiple citizenships can offer unparalleled mobility,

security, and opportunity advantages. A second passport can provide a crucial safety net in an era marked by political instability, economic fluctuations, and frequent travel restrictions.

Overview of the Benefits

1. **Travel Freedom**: With multiple passports, you can travel more freely without needing visas or access more visa-free destinations. This can save time, reduce hassle, and open up spontaneous travel opportunities.

2. **Economic Opportunities**: Different countries offer unique business environments, tax regimes, and investment opportunities. Multiple citizenships can allow you to take advantage of these diverse economic landscapes, optimizing your financial strategies.

3. **Personal Security**: Political unrest, economic crises, and natural disasters can threaten your safety and well-being. Having a second passport provides an exit strategy, ensuring

you and your family can relocate quickly and safely if necessary.

4. **Enhanced Lifestyle**: Multiple citizenships offer significant benefits, including access to better healthcare, education, and quality of life. You can live in countries that provide the best services and standards for your needs.

5. **Legacy and Future Planning**: Securing additional citizenships can be a valuable asset for your children and future generations, providing them with more opportunities and a broader perspective on the world.

Who This Book is For

This book is designed for anyone interested in expanding their horizons and enhancing global mobility. Whether you're an entrepreneur looking to tap into new markets, a digital nomad seeking more travel flexibility, or a retiree planning for a secure and enriching future, this guide will provide you with the knowledge and tools to make informed decisions about acquiring additional passports.

You may be:

- A business owner seeking to diversify your investments and reduce tax liabilities

- A professional looking to relocate for better job opportunities and quality of life

- An investor interested in citizenship-by-investment programs

- A family planning for a secure and prosperous future

- A frequent traveler wanting to avoid visa hassles

No matter your background or motivations, this book aims to demystify the process and guide you through each step with practical advice, real-life examples, and expert insights.

Embark on this journey with us as we explore the paths to global freedom, empowering you to make the most of the opportunities multiple citizenships offer. Welcome to a world without borders!

Understanding Dual and Multiple Citizenships

What is Dual Citizenship?

Dual citizenship, also known as dual nationality, refers to the status of an individual who is a legal citizen of two countries simultaneously. This means the person holds the rights and obligations associated with citizenship in both nations. These rights include living and working in either country, voting in elections, and receiving consular protection abroad. However, dual citizens must also adhere to the laws and regulations of both countries, which can sometimes present challenges.

Dual citizenship can be obtained in several ways, including by birth (if a child is born in a country that grants citizenship by birthright and to parents who are citizens of another country), through marriage, naturalization, or by descent (claiming citizenship based on the nationality of one's ancestors).

Differences Between Dual and Multiple Citizenships

While dual citizenship involves holding citizenship in two countries, multiple citizenships extends this concept further to include three or more nationalities. The key differences are primarily in the complexity and the management of rights and obligations.

1. Legal Implications:

 - **Dual Citizenship**: Involves navigating the legal systems and obligations of two countries. This might include paying taxes, fulfilling military service requirements, and understanding property ownership laws in both nations.

 - **Multiple Citizenships**: The legal implications increase with each additional citizenship. Managing the laws and regulations of three or more countries can become complex, requiring careful planning and legal assistance to ensure compliance and optimize benefits.

2. Travel and Mobility:

- **Dual Citizenship**: Provides significant travel advantages, often reducing the need for visas and facilitating easier entry into more countries.

- **Multiple Citizenships**: Expands these travel benefits even further, potentially allowing for almost seamless global mobility. This can be especially advantageous for individuals with business interests or family connections across multiple continents.

3. Economic Opportunities:

- **Dual Citizenship**: Opens up business and investment opportunities in two countries, allowing diversification of assets and income sources.

- **Multiple Citizenships**: Further broadens economic possibilities, providing access to diverse markets, tax regimes, and investment opportunities. It can also offer more strategic options for wealth management and financial planning.

4. Personal and Family Benefits:

  - **Dual Citizenship**: Enhances lifestyle options, such as access to education, healthcare, and social services in two countries.

  - **Multiple Citizenships**: This multiplication of benefits offers a wide array of choices for where to live, work, and retire. It also ensures family members enjoy the best opportunities in multiple nations.

5. Responsibilities and Obligations:

  - **Dual Citizenship**: Requires fulfilling civic duties in two countries, which can sometimes lead to conflicts of interest or dual obligations, such as military service or tax compliance.

  - **Multiple Citizenships**: Amplifies these responsibilities, necessitating a more comprehensive understanding of each country's requirements. Effective management of these obligations is crucial to avoid legal complications and maximize the benefits of multiple citizenships.

Understanding the nuances of dual and multiple citizenships is the first step toward making informed decisions about pursuing additional passports. In the following chapters, we will explore the various methods of acquiring these citizenships, their benefits, and practical strategies for managing them effectively.

Advantages and Disadvantages

Travel Freedom

One of the most significant advantages of dual and multiple citizenships is their enhanced travel freedom. With multiple passports, you have:

- **Visa-Free Travel**: Access more countries without needing a visa. This can save time and money, allowing for spontaneous travel and reducing bureaucratic hurdles.

- **Ease of Movement**: Enjoy smoother entry and exit procedures at international borders, avoiding long visa application processes and potential entry denials.

- **Consular Assistance**: Benefit from the protection and services of multiple embassies and consulates worldwide, which can be crucial in times of crisis or emergency.

Economic Opportunities

Having dual or multiple citizenships can open up a wide range of economic opportunities:

- **Investment Flexibility**: Access diverse investment opportunities in different countries, including real estate, businesses, and financial markets. This can help diversify and safeguard assets.

- **Employment Options**: Broaden your job prospects by being able to work legally in multiple countries without the need for work permits or visas.

- **Tax Optimization**: Take advantage of favorable tax regimes and incentives offered by different countries. Strategic planning can help minimize tax liabilities and optimize financial benefits.

- **Business Expansion**: Facilitate your business's expansion into new markets, benefiting from local knowledge, networks, and regulatory advantages.

Legal and Tax Implications

While there are numerous advantages to having multiple citizenships, there are also legal and tax considerations that must be managed:

- **Tax Obligations:** Dual and multiple citizens may be subject to taxation in more than one country. Understanding the tax laws, double taxation agreements, and tax planning strategies is essential to avoid unnecessary liabilities.

- **Legal Compliance**: Navigating the legal requirements of multiple countries can be complex. This includes complying with residency laws, military service obligations, and other civic duties.

- **Estate Planning**: Managing inheritance laws and estate taxes across different jurisdictions requires careful planning to ensure your assets are protected and efficiently passed on to future generations.

Potential Downsides and Challenges

While the benefits of multiple citizenships are significant, there are also potential downsides and challenges to consider:

- **Complexity**: Managing multiple citizenships' rights, obligations, and legal requirements can be complex and time-consuming. It requires careful organization and often the assistance of legal and financial advisors.

- **Conflicts of Interest**: Situations may arise where the laws or obligations of one country conflict with those of another. This can create dilemmas in military service, tax obligations, or diplomatic relations.

- **Costs**: Acquiring and maintaining multiple citizenships can be expensive. This includes application fees, legal costs, and the financial requirements for specific citizenship-by-investment programs.

- **Security Concerns**: In some cases, holding multiple citizenships can attract scrutiny or suspicion from authorities. Additionally, traveling with various passports may require careful consideration to avoid potential issues at border controls.

Understanding these advantages and disadvantages is crucial for anyone considering the pursuit of dual or Multiple Citizenships. In the following chapters, we will delve deeper into the specific methods of acquiring additional passports, the practical steps involved, and how to navigate the complexities effectively.

The Legal Landscape

International Laws and Treaties

Relevant International Agreements

Various international laws and treaties shape the legal landscape regarding dual and multiple citizenships. Understanding these agreements can help you navigate the complexities of acquiring and maintaining multiple nationalities.

1. The Universal Declaration of Human Rights (1948):

Article 15 of this declaration states that everyone has the right to a nationality and that no one shall be arbitrarily deprived of their nationality nor denied the right to change their nationality. This fundamental principle underpins the concept of dual and multiple citizenships.

2. The Hague Convention on Certain Questions Relating to the Conflict of Nationality Laws (1930):

This convention aims to reduce the incidence of statelessness and nationality conflicts. It establishes guidelines for countries to follow regarding citizenship laws, although it leaves much to the discretion of individual states.

3. The European Convention on Nationality (1997):

Adopted by the Council of Europe, this convention seeks to harmonize nationality laws among European countries. It addresses issues such as the acquisition and loss of nationality, the rights and duties of citizens, and the prevention of statelessness. While it promotes the acceptance of multiple nationalities, it also allows member states to impose restrictions.

4. Bilateral and Multilateral Agreements:

Many countries have bilateral or multilateral agreements that affect citizenship laws and the recognition of dual or multiple citizenships. These agreements can cover various issues, from tax treaties to military service obligations and citizen reciprocal rights.

How Countries Interact Regarding Citizenship

Countries have different approaches to dual and multiple citizenships, and these interactions can significantly impact your ability to acquire and maintain additional nationalities. Here's how countries typically interact on this issue:

1. **Recognition and Acceptance:**

Some countries fully recognize and accept dual and Multiple Citizenships. They allow their citizens to hold other nationalities without imposing significant restrictions or penalties. Examples include Canada, the United Kingdom, and Australia.

2. **Conditional Acceptance:**

Other countries accept dual citizenship under certain conditions. For example, they may require citizens to obtain permission before acquiring another nationality or impose restrictions on holding public office if one holds Multiple Citizenships. Examples include Germany and South Korea.

3. **Limited or No Recognition**:

Some countries do not recognize dual citizenship and require individuals to renounce their original nationality upon acquiring a new one. These countries may impose penalties or revoke citizenship if dual citizenship is discovered. Examples include India and China.

4. **Interaction in Practice**:

The practical interactions between countries regarding citizenship can vary widely. For instance, dual citizens may need to use a specific passport for entry and exit when traveling between their countries of citizenship. Additionally, issues such as tax obligations, military service, and consular protection can depend on bilateral agreements and the countries' policies.

5. **Conflict Resolution**:

In cases where the laws of two countries conflict, international agreements, and diplomatic negotiations play a crucial role in resolving issues. Dual and multiple citizens must know the potential conflicts and seek legal advice to navigate these complexities.

Understanding the international legal framework and how countries interact regarding citizenship is essential for anyone considering dual or multiple nationalities. In the following sections, we will explore country-specific laws and the various methods for acquiring additional passports.

Country-Specific Laws

Examples of Countries with Favorable Laws

Several countries have laws and policies favorable to acquiring dual or Multiple Citizenships. These countries recognize the benefits of attracting global talent and investment and fostering strong international connections.

1. **Canada:**

Canada allows dual and Multiple Citizenships. Canadian citizens are not required to renounce their citizenship when acquiring another nationality. This openness makes Canada a popular destination for immigrants and those seeking multiple passports.

2. **United Kingdom**:

The UK permits its citizens to hold dual or multiple nationalities. There are no restrictions on acquiring other citizenships, and British citizens can enjoy the benefits of being part of a global network.

3. **Portugal:**

Portugal offers several pathways to citizenship, including naturalization, descent, and investment. The country does not require new citizens to renounce their previous nationality, making it an attractive option for those seeking European Union citizenship.

4. **Australia**:

Australia recognizes dual and Multiple Citizenships. Australians can acquire additional nationalities without losing Australian citizenship, providing them with greater global mobility and opportunities.

5. **Ireland**:

Ireland allows dual and Multiple Citizenships. Its citizenship laws are relatively flexible. Irish citizenship can be acquired through birth, descent, marriage, and naturalization, making it accessible to many individuals.

Countries with Restrictions or Prohibitions

In contrast, some countries have restrictive policies regarding dual and multiple citizenships. These countries may require individuals to renounce their previous nationality or may not recognize multiple citizenships at all.

1. **India**:

India does not allow dual citizenship. Indian citizens must renounce their Indian citizenship if they acquire another nationality. However, the Overseas Citizen of India (OCI) program offers certain benefits similar to dual citizenship for former Indian citizens.

2. **China**:

China does not recognize dual citizenship. Chinese nationals who acquire a foreign nationality automatically lose their Chinese citizenship. This strict policy is aimed at maintaining national unity and control.

3. **Japan**:

Japan requires individuals to choose between Japanese citizenship and another nationality by age 22 if they hold dual citizenship at birth. Japanese law does not permit adults to maintain dual citizenship.

4. **Singapore**:

Singapore does not allow dual citizenship. Citizens who acquire another nationality must renounce their Singaporean citizenship. This policy is strictly enforced to ensure loyalty to the nation.

5. **Germany**:

Germany generally does not permit dual citizenship, although there are exceptions. For example, EU citizens and

Swiss nationals may hold dual nationality. Additionally, individuals who acquire German citizenship through naturalization may be allowed to retain their previous nationality under certain conditions.

Understanding country-specific laws is crucial for navigating the complexities of acquiring and maintaining multiple citizenships. By being aware of the favorable policies and restrictions in different countries, you can make informed decisions and strategically plan your path to global mobility and freedom.

In the next chapter, we will explore the various methods of acquiring additional passports, providing practical guidance and insights for each pathway.

Methods of Acquiring Additional Passports

Citizenship by Birth

One of the most fundamental methods of acquiring citizenship is by birth. This can occur through two primary principles: jus soli and jus sanguinis. Understanding these principles is essential for anyone considering the pathways to obtaining additional passports for themselves or their descendants.

Jus Soli (Right of the Soil)

Jus soli, or "*right of the soil*," is a principle by which a person acquires citizenship based on their birthplace. Countries that adhere to jus soli grant automatic citizenship to anyone born within their territory, regardless of their parent's nationality. This principle is pervasive in the Americas but is less prevalent in other parts of the world.

Examples of Jus Soli Countries:

1. United States:

 The U.S. grants citizenship to anyone born on its soil under the 14th Amendment to the Constitution. This includes all 50 states, the District of Columbia, and U.S. territories.

2. Canada:

 Canada follows the jus soli principle, granting citizenship to anyone born on Canadian soil, including its provinces and territories.

3. Brazil:

 Brazil provides automatic citizenship to individuals born within its borders, regardless of their parent's nationality.

Advantages of Jus Soli:

- **Automatic Citizenship**: Citizenship is granted at birth without further legal processes or documentation.

- **Broad Accessibility**: This principle allows for a straightforward path to citizenship for children born in jus soli countries, providing immediate access to the rights and benefits of that nation.

Considerations and Limitations:

- **Not Universal**: Many countries do not follow jus soli and instead base citizenship on other criteria.

- **Tourism Births**: Some countries have implemented restrictions to prevent abuse of jus soli, such as the U.S. scrutinizing "birth tourism."

Jus Sanguinis (Right of Blood)

Jus sanguinis, or "*right of blood*," is a principle by which a person acquires citizenship through their parents' nationality, regardless of their place of birth. This principle is common in many countries worldwide and allows individuals to claim citizenship based on ancestry.

Examples of Jus Sanguinis Countries:

1. **Italy:**

Italy grants citizenship to individuals with Italian ancestry. Even distant descendants of Italian citizens may be eligible to claim Italian citizenship through jus sanguinis.

2. **Ireland:**

Ireland allows individuals with Irish-born grandparents to apply for Irish citizenship. The country also recognizes more distant ancestry in some cases.

3. **Germany:**

Germany grants citizenship based on descent from German parents. The country has specific rules for individuals born to German parents abroad.

Advantages of Jus Sanguinis:

- **Ancestral Connection:** This principle allows individuals to maintain a connection to their ancestral homeland, preserving cultural and familial ties.

- **Flexibility**: Jus sanguinis provides a pathway to citizenship for individuals who may not have been born in the country but have a legitimate claim through their lineage.

Considerations and Limitations:

- **Documentation Requirements**: Claiming citizenship through jus sanguinis often requires extensive documentation, such as birth certificates, marriage certificates, and other legal records, to prove lineage.

- **Generational Limits**: Some countries impose generational limits on jus sanguinis, requiring the connection to be within a certain number of generations.

Understanding the principles of jus soli and jus sanguinis is essential for navigating the complexities of citizenship by birth. These pathways allow individuals to acquire additional passports and enjoy the benefits of multiple nationalities.

The following section will explore citizenship by descent, detailing the process of claiming citizenship based on your ancestry and the documentation required to support your application.

Citizenship by Descent

Claiming Citizenship Through Ancestry

Citizenship by descent allows individuals to acquire citizenship based on their parents' or grandparents' nationality, even if they were not born in that country. This method leverages ancestral connections to obtain a passport, making it a viable option for many seeking dual or multiple citizenships.

Countries Offering Citizenship by Descent:

1. **Italy:**

   Italy offers citizenship to individuals with Italian ancestors. Even if your ancestors emigrated several generations ago, you might still be eligible. Italian citizenship by descent can be passed down without generational limits, provided the lineage is unbroken.

2. **Ireland:**

   Ireland allows individuals with Irish-born grandparents to apply for Irish citizenship. Even great-grandparents' connections can sometimes qualify, notably if the intermediate generation registers the birth with the Foreign Births Register.

3. **Poland:**

Poland grants citizenship to descendants of Polish nationals, particularly those who left Poland before the end of World War II. This includes the descendants of emigrants who fled political or economic turmoil.

Advantages of Citizenship by Descent:

- **Heritage and Identity**: Acquiring citizenship through descent allows individuals to connect with their ancestral heritage and cultural identity.

- **Rights and Benefits**: Citizenship by descent often grants full rights and benefits, including the ability to live, work, and study in the country of your ancestors.

- **E.U. Access**: For countries within the European Union, citizenship by descent can provide access to the entire E.U., including the right to live and work in any member state.

Required Documentation and Processes

Claiming citizenship by descent typically involves a detailed application process with specific documentation requirements. The exact requirements vary by country, but the following documents are commonly needed:

1. Birth Certificates:

Provide your birth certificate and those of your ancestors (parents, grandparents) to establish the lineage. Certified copies and translations may be required.

2. Marriage Certificates:

If applicable, provide your parents' or grandparents' marriage certificates to verify the continuity of the family line.

3. Proof of Nationality:

Documents proving the nationality of your ancestors, such as their passports, naturalization certificates, or citizenship records.

4. **Historical Records**:

Depending on the country, you may need additional historical records, such as immigration documents, census records, or military service records, to demonstrate your ancestral connection.

5. **Personal Identification**:

Provide copies of your identification documents, such as your current passport, national I.D. card, and proof of residence.

Application Process:

1. **Research Eligibility**:

Begin by researching the specific requirements and eligibility criteria for citizenship by descent in the country of your ancestors. Official government websites and consulates are good starting points.

2. **Gather Documentation**:

Collect all necessary documents, ensuring they are certified and translated if required. This step may involve reaching out to government archives, family members, or professional genealogists.

3. **Submit Application**:

Complete the application forms provided by the relevant authorities. Submit the forms and supporting documentation to the appropriate government office, consulate, or embassy.

4. **Await Processing**:

Processing times vary by country, ranging from a few months to several years. Be prepared for potential delays and requests for additional information.

5. **Approval and Citizenship**:

Upon approval, you will be granted citizenship and issued a passport. Some countries may require you to attend an interview or take an oath of allegiance.

6. **Maintain Compliance**:

Stay informed about any requirements for maintaining citizenship, such as renewal procedures, residency obligations, or dual citizenship regulations.

Understanding the process and requirements for citizenship by descent is crucial for successfully acquiring additional passports. In the next section, we will explore naturalization, a common pathway for those who establish residency in a new country and wish to become citizens through legal means.

Naturalization

Naturalization is a process through which a foreign national can acquire citizenship of a country after meeting specific legal requirements. This method is commonly used by individuals who have established residency in a new country and wish to become citizens through legal means.

Requirements and Process

The requirements for naturalization vary by country but generally include the following:

1. Residency Requirement:

Most countries require a period of continuous residence within their borders before an individual can apply for naturalization. The length of this period can vary significantly, typically ranging from 3 to 10 years.

2. Legal Status:

Applicants must hold legal residency status in the country, such as a permanent residence visa, work visa, or other qualifying status.

3. Language Proficiency:

Many countries require applicants to demonstrate proficiency in the national language. This often involves passing a language test to ensure the applicant can effectively communicate and integrate into society.

4. Civic Knowledge:

Applicants may need to pass a test on the country's history, government, and civic values. This ensures new citizens understand and respect the nation's heritage and legal framework.

5. Good Character:

A background check is usually conducted to verify the applicant's good character. This includes reviewing criminal records, financial history, and overall conduct.

6. Financial Stability:

Some countries require proof of financial stability, ensuring applicants can support themselves and their dependents without relying on public assistance.

7. Oath of Allegiance:

Upon approval, applicants must take an oath of allegiance, pledging loyalty to their new country and its laws.

Application Process:

1. Research Eligibility:

Begin by researching the specific naturalization requirements and eligibility criteria for the country where you seek citizenship. Official government websites and immigration offices provide the most accurate information.

2. Gather Documentation:

Collect all necessary documents, such as proof of residency, language proficiency certificates, financial statements, and personal identification. Ensure these documents are certified and translated if required.

3. Submit Application:

Complete the naturalization application forms and submit them with all supporting documentation to the appropriate government office or immigration authority.

4. Attend Interviews and Tests:

Be prepared to attend interviews, language tests, and civic knowledge exams during the evaluation process. These steps assess your integration into the country's society and adherence to its values.

5. Await Decision:

Processing times for naturalization applications can vary, often taking several months to a few years. During this period, immigration authorities will review your application, conduct background checks, and verify your eligibility.

6. Approval and Oath Ceremony:

If your application is approved, you will be invited to an oath ceremony where you will pledge allegiance to your new country. This is the final step in becoming a naturalized citizen.

7. Receive Citizenship and Passport:

After the oath ceremony, you will be issued a naturalization certificate, officially granting citizenship. You can then apply for a passport, allowing you to enjoy the rights and benefits of your new nationality.

Timeframes and Residency Requirements

The timeframe for naturalization and the residency requirements can vary widely by country. Here are some common timeframe examples:

1. **United States**:

   - Residency Requirement: 5 years (3 years if married to a U.S. citizen)

   - Additional Requirements: Continuous residence, physical presence, English proficiency, and knowledge of U.S. history and government

2. **Canada**:

   - Residency Requirement: 3 years (1,095 days) within the last five years

- Additional Requirements: Language proficiency in English or French, knowledge of Canada's history, values, institutions, and symbols

3. **Australia**:

- Residency Requirement: 4 years of lawful residence, including one year as a permanent resident

- Additional Requirements: Good character, basic knowledge of English, understanding of Australian values

4. **United Kingdom**:

- Residency Requirement: 5 years (3 years if married to a British citizen)

- Additional Requirements: Knowledge of English, Welsh, or Scottish Gaelic, Life in the U.K. test, good character

5. **Germany**:

- Residency Requirement: 8 years (reduced to 7 years with integration course)

- Additional Requirements: Proficiency in German, knowledge of German legal and social system, financial stability, renouncement of previous citizenship (with some exceptions)

Understanding the requirements and processes for naturalization is essential for successfully acquiring citizenship through this method. The following section will explore citizenship by marriage, detailing how marital relationships can provide a pathway to additional passports and the specific criteria involved.

Citizenship by Marriage

Marrying a citizen of another country can provide a pathway to acquiring citizenship in that country. Many nations offer streamlined naturalization processes for foreign spouses, recognizing the familial and social integration that marriage represents. However, the specific eligibility requirements and procedures can vary significantly between countries.

Eligibility and Process

1. Eligibility Criteria:

- *Marriage to a Citizen*: The primary requirement is being legally married to a citizen of the country where you seek citizenship. This marriage must be recognized under the laws of that country.

- *Duration of Marriage*: Many countries require that the marriage be of a specific duration before you can apply for citizenship. This period can range from one to several years.

- *Residency Requirement*: Some countries require that you live in the country with your spouse for a specified period before applying for citizenship. This residency requirement ensures that the marriage is genuine and you have integrated into the local community.

- *Proof of Genuine Relationship*: You may need to provide evidence that your marriage is genuine and not solely to obtain citizenship. This can include joint financial accounts, shared property, photographs, and affidavits from family and friends.

2. **Application Process**:

  - ***Gather Documentation***: Collect all necessary documents, including your marriage certificate, proof of your spouse's citizenship, and evidence of your relationship. Ensure these documents are certified and translated if required.

  - ***Submit Application***: Complete the citizenship application forms and submit them along with all supporting documentation to the appropriate government office or immigration authority.

  - ***Interviews and Background Checks***: Be prepared for interviews and background checks. Immigration authorities may interview you and your spouse to verify the authenticity of your marriage and assess your integration into society.

  - ***Language and Civic Knowledge***: Some countries require you to demonstrate proficiency in the local language and knowledge of the country's history and culture. This may involve taking language tests and attending citizenship classes.

  - ***Await Decision***: Processing times can vary, and you may need to wait several months to a few years for a decision. During this period, authorities will review your application, conduct background checks, and verify your eligibility.

- *Approval and Oath Ceremony*: If your application is approved, you may be invited to an oath ceremony where you pledge allegiance to your new country. This is the final step in becoming a naturalized citizen through marriage.

- *Receive Citizenship and Passport*: After the oath ceremony, you will be issued a naturalization certificate, officially granting you citizenship. You can then apply for a passport, allowing you to enjoy the rights and benefits of your new nationality.

Benefits and Potential Pitfalls

Benefits:

- *Streamlined Process*: Citizenship by marriage often involves a more straightforward and faster naturalization process than other methods. The relationship with a citizen provides a clear path to integration and acceptance.

- *Family Unity*: This method supports family unity by allowing spouses to live and build their lives together in the same country without prolonged separation or complex immigration hurdles.

- *Cultural Integration*: Living with a local spouse can enhance cultural integration, helping you learn the language, customs, and societal norms more effectively.

- *Enhanced Rights and Benefits*: Acquiring citizenship through marriage grants you the same rights and benefits as any other citizen, including the ability to live, work, and study in the country.

Potential Pitfalls:

- *Scrutiny and Verification*: Authorities often scrutinize applications for citizenship by marriage to prevent fraudulent marriages. This can involve intrusive interviews and investigations into your personal life.

- *Residency Requirements*: Some countries impose strict residency requirements, meaning you must live in the country with your spouse for a certain period. It can be challenging if you have career or family obligations elsewhere.

- *Dependency on Relationship*: Your path to citizenship is tied to the stability of your marriage. If the marriage ends before the naturalization process is complete, you may lose your eligibility for citizenship.

- *Cultural and Legal Adjustments*: Moving to a new country and adapting to different cultural and legal systems can be challenging. It requires flexibility, patience, and a willingness to integrate into a new environment.

Understanding the eligibility and process for citizenship by marriage is crucial for acquiring additional passports through this method. The next section will explore economic citizenship, detailing how investment programs can provide a pathway to citizenship and the specific criteria involved.

Economic Citizenship

Economic citizenship, also known as citizenship by investment (CBI) or residency by investment (RBI), is a method by which individuals can acquire citizenship or residency in a country by making a significant financial investment. It is a pathway that attracts high-net-worth individuals seeking greater global mobility, tax advantages, and enhanced personal security.

Citizenship by Investment (CBI):

CBI programs offer direct citizenship to individuals who make qualifying investments in the country. These investments can take various forms, including:

1. **Real Estate Investment**:

- Purchasing property in the country. The investment amount and types of qualifying properties vary by country.

- Example: Saint Kitts and Nevis requires a minimum real estate investment of $200,000 in government-approved projects.

2. **Government Bonds or Donations**:

- Investing in government bonds or making a non-refundable donation to a government fund.

- Example: Dominica offers citizenship in exchange for a donation of $100,000 to the Economic Diversification Fund.

3. **Business Investment**:

- Investing in or starting a business that creates jobs and contributes to the economy.

- Example: Malta requires an investment in a business that benefits the local economy and other financial contributions.

Residency by Investment (RBI):

RBI programs provide residency status, which can lead to citizenship after a certain period. These programs typically require:

1. **Real Estate Investment**:

   - Purchasing property to gain residency rights.

   - Example: Portugal's Golden Visa program requires a minimum real estate investment of €500,000.

2. **Capital Investment**:

   - Investing in local companies, government bonds, or financial instruments.

   - Example: Spain's Golden Visa program requires an investment of €2 million in Spanish government bonds.

3. **Job Creation**:

- Establishing a business that creates jobs for local residents.

- Example: The United States EB-5 Immigrant Investor Program requires an investment of $900,000 to $1.8 million in a commercial enterprise that creates at least ten full-time jobs.

Costs and Benefits

Costs:

- *Financial Outlay*: The primary cost of economic citizenship is the investment, ranging from hundreds of thousands to millions of dollars. In addition, there may be government fees, due diligence fees, and legal costs.

- *Maintenance Costs*: Real estate investments may involve maintenance and property management expenses. Some countries also require periodic renewals and associated fees.

- *Non-Refundable Contributions*: Donations to government funds are typically non-refundable, representing a sunk cost for applicants.

Benefits:

- *Quick and Efficient Process*: CBI programs often provide a faster route to citizenship than traditional naturalization processes. In some cases, citizenship can be granted within a few months.

- *Global Mobility*: Economic citizenship can significantly enhance travel freedom, offering visa-free or visa-on-arrival access to numerous countries.

- *Tax Optimization*: Some countries with CBI programs offer favorable tax regimes, allowing investors to optimize their tax liabilities and protect their wealth.

- *Personal and Family Security*: Economic citizenship provides a safety net for individuals and their families, offering an alternative residence during political or economic instability.

- *Economic Opportunities*: Investors gain access to new markets and business opportunities, benefiting from the host country's economic environment and legal protections.

- *Inclusion of Family Members*: Many CBI programs allow applicants to include family members in their application, extending the benefits of citizenship to spouses, children, and sometimes parents.

Popular CBI Programs:

1. Saint Kitts and Nevis:

- Known for its long-established CBI program, offering citizenship through real estate investment or donation to the Sustainable Growth Fund.

- Benefits include visa-free travel to over 150 countries.

2. Malta:

- Offers citizenship through a combination of real estate investment, financial contributions, and residency requirements.

- Benefits include access to the European Union and visa-free travel within the Schengen Area.

3. Portugal:

- Provides a Golden Visa program that grants residency through real estate or capital investment and provides a pathway to citizenship after five years.

- Benefits include visa-free travel within the Schengen Area and the right to live, work, and study in Portugal.

4. **Cyprus**:

  - Offers citizenship through significant real estate or business investment.

  - Benefits include E.U. citizenship and visa-free travel to over 170 countries.

5. **Dominica**:

  - Offers a straightforward and cost-effective CBI program through real estate investment or donation to the Economic Diversification Fund.

  - Benefits include visa-free travel to over 140 countries.

Understanding the various economic citizenship programs, costs, and benefits is crucial for making an informed decision about acquiring additional passports through investment. In the next section, we will explore special programs, including asylum, refugee status, and honorary citizenship, detailing the unique pathways they offer to acquiring additional nationalities.

Special Programs

In addition to the more common pathways to citizenship, several special programs can also lead to acquiring additional passports. These include asylum and refugee status, exceptional cases, and honorary citizenship.

Asylum and Refugee Status

Asylum and refugee status provide protection and a pathway to citizenship for individuals fleeing persecution, violence, or severe instability in their home countries. These programs are based on humanitarian grounds and are governed by international laws and agreements.

1. **Asylum Seekers**:

   - Asylum seekers apply for protection in a foreign country because they fear persecution due to race, religion, nationality, membership in a particular social group, or political opinion.

   - The process typically involves applying for asylum upon arrival in the host country or at its borders. Applicants must prove they have a well-founded fear of persecution if they return to their home country.

2. **Refugees**:

- Refugees are individuals who a foreign country or international organization has granted protection after being forced to flee their home country due to conflict, persecution, or other serious threats.

- Refugee status is often determined by the United Nations High Commissioner for Refugees (UNHCR) or the host country's asylum system.

Pathway to Citizenship:

- *Temporary Protection*: Initially, asylum seekers and refugees are granted temporary protection, which includes the right to stay and access to essential services.

- *Permanent Residency*: After a certain period, often ranging from 3 to 5 years, individuals may apply for permanent residency.

- *Naturalization*: Permanent residents can eventually apply for citizenship, provided they meet the host country's residency, language, and integration requirements.

Benefits and Challenges:

- *Benefits*: It provides safety, legal protection, and access to essential services. Eventually, it offers a pathway to citizenship and a new life in a stable environment.

- *Challenges*: The application process can be lengthy and complex, requiring substantial evidence of persecution. Asylum seekers and refugees often face legal and social challenges during the integration process.

Exceptional Cases and Honorary Citizenship

In certain circumstances, countries may grant citizenship to individuals based on exceptional cases or honorary recognition. These are rare and typically involve extraordinary contributions or achievements.

1. Exceptional Cases:

- Citizenship may be granted to individuals who have made significant contributions to the country in fields such as science, technology, culture, sports, or philanthropy.

- Governments may use their discretionary powers to grant citizenship to individuals who bring substantial economic, social, or cultural benefits to the nation.

Examples:

- *Scientific Contributions*: A renowned scientist or researcher who has significantly advanced the country's scientific knowledge or technological capabilities.

- *Cultural Achievements*: An artist, musician, or writer whose work has profoundly impacted the country's cultural landscape.

2. **Honorary Citizenship**:

- Honorary citizenship is a symbolic status awarded to individuals who have rendered exceptional service or honor to a country. It does not necessarily grant the full legal rights and privileges of regular citizenship.

- National or local governments often bestow this recognition to honor distinguished individuals, such as foreign dignitaries, philanthropists, or cultural icons.

Examples:

- *International Leaders*: Foreign leaders or diplomats who have fostered strong bilateral relations and cooperation between their home country and the host country.

- *Humanitarians*: Individuals who have made outstanding humanitarian contributions, benefiting the host country or the global community.

Benefits and Limitations:

- **Benefits:** Provides recognition and symbolic association with the host country. In some cases, it may grant legal rights and privileges similar to those of regular citizens.

- **Limitations:** Honorary citizenship is mainly symbolic and may not include legal citizenship's full rights and obligations. Exceptional case citizenship, while more comprehensive, is rarely granted and subject to stringent criteria.

Understanding these unique programs can provide additional avenues for acquiring citizenship in unique circumstances. While these pathways are less common, they offer valuable options for individuals facing exceptional situations or seeking recognition for their contributions.

In the next chapter, we will explore popular countries for second citizenship, highlighting their programs, benefits, and requirements to help you decide where to seek additional passports.

Popular Countries for Second Citizenship

Caribbean Nations

The Caribbean nations are well-known for their attractive citizenship by investment (CBI) programs. These countries offer relatively straightforward and efficient pathways to citizenship, often with the added benefit of visa-free travel to numerous countries. Here's an overview of the CBI programs offered by Dominica, St. Kitts and Nevis, and Antigua and Barbuda.

Dominica

Dominica's Citizenship by Investment Program is one of the most cost-effective and popular in the Caribbean. Established in 1993, it offers several pathways to acquiring citizenship.

Investment Options:

1. **Economic Diversification Fund (EDF)**:

 - A non-refundable donation to the EDF, which supports public and private sector projects in Dominica.

 - Minimum Contribution: $200,000 for a single applicant.

2. **Real Estate Investment**:

 - Purchase of government-approved real estate, which must be held for at least three years.

 - Minimum Investment: $200,000.

Benefits:

- *Visa-Free Travel*: Visa-free or visa-on-arrival access to over 140 countries, including the Schengen Area, the UK, and Hong Kong.

- *Quick Processing*: Citizenship can be obtained within 3 to 6 months.

- *No Residency Requirement*: Applicants are not required to reside in Dominica before or after obtaining citizenship.

St. Kitts and Nevis

St. Kitts and Nevis has one of the longest-running CBI programs in the world, established in 1984. It is known for its stability and reliability.

Investment Options:

1. **Sustainable Growth Fund (SGF):**

   - A non-refundable donation to the SGF, which supports economic growth and sustainable development projects.

   - Minimum Contribution: $200,000 for a single applicant.

2. **Real Estate Investment:**

   - Purchase of government-approved real estate, which must be held for at least five years.

   - Minimum Investment: $200,000 (shared ownership) or $400,000 (full ownership).

Benefits:

- *Visa-Free Travel*: Visa-free or visa-on-arrival access to over 150 countries, including the Schengen Area, the UK, and Singapore.

- *Quick Processing*: Citizenship can be obtained within 3 to 6 months.

- *No Residency Requirement*: Applicants are not required to reside in St. Kitts and Nevis before or after obtaining citizenship.

Antigua and Barbuda

Antigua and Barbuda's Citizenship by Investment Program, established in 2013, offers several investment options and provides a balanced combination of benefits and requirements.

Investment Options:

1. **National Development Fund (NDF):**

   - A non-refundable donation to the NDF, which supports national development projects.

   - Minimum Contribution: $200,000 for a single applicant or a family of four.

2. **Real Estate Investment:**

- Purchase of government-approved real estate, which must be held for at least five years.

- Minimum Investment: $200,000.

3. **Business Investment**:

- Investment in an approved business, either as a sole investor or as part of a joint venture.

- Minimum Investment: $1.5 million (sole) or $400,000 (joint venture, with a total investment of $5 million).

Benefits:

- *Visa-Free Travel*: Visa-free or visa-on-arrival access to over 150 countries, including the Schengen Area, the UK, and Canada.

- *Quick Processing*: Citizenship can be obtained within 3 to 6 months.

- *Residency Requirement*: Applicants must spend at least five days in Antigua and Barbuda within the first five years of citizenship.

The Caribbean nations offer attractive citizenship by investment programs with various benefits, making them popular choices for individuals seeking second citizenship.

In the next section, we will explore European options for second citizenship, highlighting the programs offered by Portugal, Malta, and Cyprus.

European Options

Europe offers several attractive options for acquiring second citizenship through investment programs. Portugal, Malta, and Cyprus have well-established pathways that provide numerous benefits, including access to the European Union and enhanced global mobility. Here's an overview of the citizenship by investment (CBI) and residency by investment (RBI) programs offered by these countries.

Portugal

Portugal's Golden Visa program is one of Europe's most popular residency by investment schemes. It offers a pathway to citizenship after a period of residency and investment.

Investment Options:

1. **Real Estate Investment:**

   - Purchase real estate with a minimum value of €500,000 for properties in low-density areas or those requiring renovation.

2. **Capital Transfer:**

   - Transfer of at least €1 million into a Portuguese bank account or approved investment.

3. **Business and Job Creation:**

   - Investment of €350,000 in research activities or creation of at least ten jobs.

Benefits:

- *Visa-Free Travel*: Visa-free access to the Schengen Area.

- *Pathway to Citizenship*: Applicants can apply for Portuguese citizenship after five years of residency, provided they meet language and residency requirements.

- *No Residency Requirement*: Only requires an average stay of seven days per year.

Malta

Malta offers a citizenship-by-investment program known as the Malta Individual Investor Program (MIIP), which provides a direct route to citizenship within a relatively short timeframe. However, the total is close to one million euros with all investments and donations required.

Investment Options:

1. **Contribution to National Development and Social Fund (NDSF):**

   - A non-refundable contribution of €650,000 for the principal applicant, €25,000 for a spouse and each minor child, and €50,000 for each dependent adult child or parent.

2. **Real Estate Investment:**

   - Purchase property valued at a minimum of €350,000 or lease property with an annual rental value of at least €16,000, to be held for five years.

3. **Government Bonds or Shares:**

   - Investment of at least €150,000 in government-approved bonds or shares, to be held for five years.

Benefits:

- *EU Citizenship*: Full citizenship with the right to live, work, and study in any EU country.

- *Visa-Free Travel*: Visa-free or visa-on-arrival access to over 180 countries, including the USA, Canada, and the UK.

- *Quick Processing*: Citizenship can be obtained within 12 to 14 months.

Cyprus

Cyprus offers a straightforward citizenship-by-investment program, which is particularly attractive due to its relatively short residency requirement and substantial benefits.

Investment Options:

1. **Real Estate Investment:**

   - Purchase real estate with a minimum value of €2 million, including residential or commercial properties.

2. Business Investment:

   - Investment of €2 million in Cypriot businesses or companies, creating at least five jobs for Cypriot citizens.

3. Government Bonds:

   - Investment in government bonds with a maximum limit of €500,000 as part of the total investment requirement.

Benefits:

- *EU Citizenship*: Full citizenship with the right to live, work, and study in any EU country.

- *Visa-Free Travel*: Visa-free or visa-on-arrival access to over 170 countries, including the Schengen Area, Canada, and the UK.

- *No Residency Requirement*: No physical residency requirement before or after obtaining citizenship.

These European options offer diverse pathways to acquiring second citizenship through investment, each with benefits and requirements. In the next section, we will explore options in the Americas, focusing on Canada, Mexico, and Panama, and their respective pathways to second citizenship.

The Americas

The Americas offer various attractive options for acquiring second citizenship, each with unique benefits and requirements. Canada, Mexico, and Panama provide citizenship pathways through residency programs catering to different needs, from economic opportunities to lifestyle preferences.

Canada

Canada is known for its welcoming immigration policies and high quality of life. While Canada does not offer direct citizenship through an investment program, it has several pathways through which individuals can obtain permanent residency, which can eventually lead to citizenship.

Investment Options:

1. **Quebec Immigrant Investor Program (QIIP)**:

 - Requires an investment of CAD 1.2 million in a government-guaranteed investment for five years.

- Applicants must have a minimum net worth of CAD 2 million and management experience.

2. **Start-Up Visa Program**:

 - Requires a commitment from a designated Canadian venture capital fund, angel investor group, or business incubator.

 - No specific investment amount, but the business must be innovative, create jobs, and compete globally.

3. **Provincial Nominee Programs (PNPs)**:

 - Various provinces offer PNPs tailored to entrepreneurs and investors, with varying investment requirements and criteria.

Benefits:

- *Pathway to Citizenship*: Permanent residents can apply for citizenship within five years after three years of residency.

- *High Quality of Life*: Access to excellent healthcare, education, and a safe, multicultural environment.

- *Global Mobility*: Canadian citizens enjoy visa-free or visa-on-arrival access to over 180 countries.

Mexico

Mexico's residency programs offer a relatively straightforward path to citizenship, appealing to retirees, investors, and entrepreneurs alike.

Investment Options:

1. **Temporary Resident Visa**:

   - Requires proof of monthly income of approximately USD 2,000 or bank account balance of around USD 80,000.

   - Can be renewed for up to four years, after which applicants can apply for permanent residency.

2. **Permanent Resident Visa**:

   - Requires a higher income proof or bank balance than a temporary visa or investment in Mexican real estate or businesses.

3. **Real Estate Investment**:

   - Investment in Mexican real estate worth approximately USD 200,000 or more can qualify for residency.

Benefits:

- *Pathway to Citizenship*: Permanent residents can apply for citizenship after five years of residency.

- *Cost of Living*: Mexico offers a lower living cost than many Western countries.

- *Proximity*: proximity to the United States and Canada, with excellent travel connections.

Panama

Panama's Friendly Nations Visa and favorable tax environment make it a popular choice for those seeking second citizenship.

Investment Options:

1. **Friendly Nations Visa:**

   - Requires establishing a business or making a real estate investment of at least USD 200,000.

   - Available to citizens of over 50 designated "*friendly*" countries.

2. **Qualified Investor Program**:

 - Investment of USD 500,000 in real estate, a fixed-term deposit in a local bank, or government securities.

 - Accelerated processing time for residency.

3. **Retiree (Pensionado) Program**:

 - Requires proof of a lifetime monthly pension of at least USD 1,000.

 - Offers immediate permanent residency with various benefits.

Benefits:

- *Pathway to Citizenship*: Permanent residents can apply for citizenship after five years of residency.

- *Tax Advantages*: No taxes on foreign-earned income, making it an attractive option for retirees and business owners.

- *High Quality of Life*: Modern amenities, excellent healthcare, and a warm climate.

These American options provide diverse pathways to acquiring second citizenship through investment and residency programs. Each country offers unique benefits that cater to different needs and preferences. In the next section, we will explore options in Asia and the Pacific, focusing on Singapore, New Zealand, and Vanuatu and their respective pathways to second citizenship.

Asia and Pacific

The Asia-Pacific region offers several appealing options for acquiring second citizenship, each with distinct pathways and benefits. Singapore, New Zealand, and Vanuatu provide attractive opportunities for investors, entrepreneurs, and those seeking a higher quality of life.

Singapore

Singapore is renowned for its strong economy, excellent infrastructure, and high standard of living. While it does not have a direct citizenship by investment program, its residency schemes offer a pathway to citizenship.

Investment Options:

1. **Global Investor Program (GIP):**

 - Investment of at least SGD 2.5 million in a new business entity or expansion of an existing business in Singapore.

 - Alternatively, invest SGD 2.5 million in a GIP-approved fund in Singapore-based companies.

2. **EntrePass:**

 - Designed for entrepreneurs who want to start and operate a business in Singapore.

 - Requires innovative business ideas and plans, with no specific investment amount, but significant business activity and job creation are expected.

Benefits:

- *Pathway to Citizenship*: Permanent residents can apply for citizenship after two years of residency.

- *Economic Opportunities*: Access to a thriving business environment and strategic location for regional operations.

- *High Standard of Living*: Excellent healthcare, education, safety, and a cosmopolitan lifestyle.

New Zealand

New Zealand offers a high quality of life, stunning natural landscapes, and a welcoming environment for investors and entrepreneurs. The country provides several pathways to residency, leading to citizenship.

Investment Options:

1. **Investor Visa (Investor 1 Category):**

   - Investment of NZD 10 million in New Zealand over three years.

   - No age limit, language requirement, or business experience needed.

2. **Investor Visa (Investor 2 Category):**

   - Investment of NZD 3 million over four years.

- Requires applicants to be under 65 years old, have at least three years of business experience, and meet English language requirements.

3. **Entrepreneur Work Visa:**

   - Requires a minimum capital investment of NZD 100,000 in a New Zealand business.

   - Points-based system considering age, business experience, and job creation.

Benefits:

- *Pathway to Citizenship*: Permanent residents can apply for citizenship after five years of residency.

- *Quality of Life*: High healthcare, education, personal safety standards, and a clean and green environment.

- *Economic Stability*: Access to a stable economy with opportunities in various sectors, including technology, agriculture, and tourism.

Vanuatu

Vanuatu offers one of the world's fastest and most affordable citizenship-by-investment programs. It is an attractive option for those seeking quick and easy access to a second passport.

Investment Options:

1. **Development Support Program (DSP):**

  - Non-refundable donation of USD 130,000 for a single applicant, USD 150,000 for a couple, and higher amounts for larger families.

  - The funds support various development projects in Vanuatu.

Benefits:

- *Quick Processing:* Citizenship can be obtained within 1 to 2 months.

- *Visa-Free Travel:* Visa-free or visa-on-arrival access to over 130 countries, including the UK, Schengen Area, and Hong Kong.

- No Residency Requirement: No requirement to reside in Vanuatu before or after obtaining citizenship.

These options in Asia and the Pacific offer diverse pathways to acquiring second citizenship, catering to different needs and preferences. Each country provides unique benefits, from economic opportunities and high standards of living to quick and affordable processes. In the next chapter, we will explore the application process, detailing the steps involved in gathering necessary documents, filling out applications, and navigating interviews and background checks.

The Application Process

Gathering Necessary Documents

Applying for second citizenship involves meticulous preparation and gathering various essential documents. The specific requirements may vary depending on the country and the type of investment or residency program you are applying for. However, some standard documents are typically required across most programs. Here's a detailed look at the key documents you'll need.

Birth Certificates

What You Need:

1. **Applicant's Birth Certificate:**

   - A certified copy of your birth certificate is generally required. Some will want the certificate to have both your parent's names on it. This document verifies your identity and date of birth.

2. **Spouse's Birth Certificate**:

   - If you are applying with your spouse, their birth certificate will also be required.

3. **Children's Birth Certificates**:

   - Their birth certificates, including dependent children, are necessary for applications to prove your relationship and their ages.

Why It's Needed:

- Birth certificates establish identity, familial relationships, and eligibility based on age or dependency status.

Tips:

- Ensure all birth certificates are in the required format, typically certified copies.

- If the original documents are not in the host country's official language, obtain certified translations.

Proof of Residence

What You Need:

1. **Current Proof of Residence**:

   - Recent utility bills, bank statements, or rental agreements that show your current address.

2. **Residency Permits**:

   - If you are already a resident of the country where you are applying for citizenship, you must provide copies of your residency permits.

Why It's Needed:

- Proof of residence is used to confirm your current living situation and establish your presence in the country if required by the program.

Tips:

- Ensure the documents are recent, typically within the last three months.

- Multiple forms of proof may be required, so gather various documents.

Financial Statements

What You Need:

1. **Bank Statements:**

   - Recent bank statements from all your accounts. These statements show your financial stability and ability to make the required investment.

2. **Investment Records**:

   - Proof of any investments you have made, such as property deeds, stock certificates, or business ownership documents.

3. **Tax Returns**:

  - Recent tax returns may be required to verify your income and financial status.

Why It's Needed:

- Financial statements demonstrate your financial capacity to meet the investment or donation requirements of the citizenship program.

Tips:

- Gather bank statements covering the last six to twelve months.

- Ensure all financial documents are official and clearly show account details and balances.

- For investment records, ensure you have proof of purchase and current value.

Additional Documents:

Depending on the specific program, additional documents may also be required. These can include:

1. **Police Clearance Certificates**:

   - To demonstrate good character and absence of a criminal record. Obtain from all countries where you have lived for a significant period.

2. **Medical Reports**:

   - Some countries require a medical examination to ensure you do not have any communicable diseases or significant health issues.

3. **Marriage Certificate**:

   - If applying with a spouse, provide a certified copy of your marriage certificate.

4. **Passports:**

   - Copies of your current passport(s) will be used to verify your identity and travel history. In many cases, they will want copies of every page in your passport.

General Tips for Document Preparation:

- **Certification and Translation**: Ensure all documents are certified and, if necessary, translated into the host country's official language by a certified translator.

- **Organization**: Keep all documents organized in logical order, preferably in a dedicated folder or binder.

- **Backup Copies**: Make copies of all documents for your records and submission, if required.

- **Timeliness**: Ensure all documents are current and obtained within the timeframe specified by the citizenship program.

Gathering the necessary documents is a critical step in the application process for second citizenship. The next section will explore the steps in filling out applications, including common forms, requirements, and tips for avoiding common mistakes.

Filling Out Applications

Successfully applying for second citizenship requires meticulous attention to detail when filling out the necessary application forms. Here's a guide to understanding common forms, requirements, as well as tips for avoiding common mistakes.

Common Forms and Requirements

1. **Application Form**:

> ➢ Personal Information: Basic details such as your full name, date of birth, place of birth, and current nationality.

> ➢ Family Information: Details about your spouse, children, and other dependents, including names, dates of birth, and current nationalities.

> ➢ Contact Information: Your current address, phone number, and email address.

> ➢ Employment History: Information about your current and previous employment, including job titles, company names, and durations.

> ➢ Educational Background: Details of your qualifications, including institutions attended, degrees obtained, and dates.

> ➢ Investment Details: Information about the type and amount of investment you are making to qualify for citizenship, such as real estate, government bonds, or business investments.

> ➢ Residency Information: Your current residency status, past addresses, and prior residency permits.

2. **Supporting Documents**:

- ➤ Proof of Identity: Passports, national IDs, and birth certificates.
- ➤ Proof of Marital Status: Marriage certificates, divorce decrees, or death certificates of a spouse if applicable.
- ➤ Financial Documents: Bank statements, investment records, tax returns, and financial affidavits.
- ➤ Police Clearance Certificates: From all countries where you have lived for a significant period.
- ➤ Medical Certificates: Health checks to confirm the absence of infectious diseases or significant health issues.

3. **Affidavits and Declarations**:

- ➤ Background and Character Declarations: Statements affirming that you have no criminal record and are of good character.
- ➤ Commitment to Investment: Declarations confirming your commitment to maintaining the required investment for the specified period.
- ➤ Oath of Allegiance: A pledge to uphold the laws and values of the new country, usually required at the final stage of the application process.

Tips for Avoiding Common Mistakes

1. **Double-Check Information**:

   - Accuracy: Ensure that all information provided is accurate and matches the details in your supporting documents. Inconsistent or incorrect information can lead to delays or rejections.

   - Completeness: Fill out all sections of the application form completely. Do not leave any fields blank unless specifically instructed.

2. **Follow Instructions**:

   - Guidelines: Carefully read and follow the application guidelines provided by the citizenship program. Each country may have specific requirements and instructions.

   - Document Format: Ensure that documents are provided in the required format, such as certified copies, notarized documents, and translated versions if necessary.

3. **Use Professional Help**:

   - Legal and Financial Advisors: Consider hiring immigration lawyers or consultants who specialize in citizenship by investment programs. They can provide valuable assistance and ensure your application is correctly filled out.

- Certified Translators: Use certified translators for documents outside the host country's official language to avoid issues with document acceptance.

4. **Prepare Thoroughly**:

- Document Checklist: Use a checklist to ensure that you have gathered all required documents. Double-check that each document is current, certified, and translated as needed.

- Photocopies: Make photocopies of all documents for your records and submission if multiple copies are required.

5. **Address Issues Promptly**:

- Clarifications: If you are unsure about any part of the application or requirements, seek clarification from the relevant authorities or legal advisor.

- Corrections: Promptly address any errors or omissions identified during the review process. Submit corrected information as quickly as possible to avoid delays.

6. **Keep Track of Deadlines**:

- Submission Deadlines: Be aware of application deadlines and ensure that all materials are submitted on time.

- Renewal Deadlines: Keep track of residency or investment renewal deadlines to maintain eligibility.

7. **Stay Organized**:

- Application Folder: Maintain a dedicated folder or digital file for all application materials, including forms, supporting documents, correspondence, and receipts.

- Updates: Keep a record of any updates or communications from the authorities handling your application.

Filling out applications accurately and thoroughly is crucial to the success of your citizenship application. In the next section, we will explore the steps involved in interviews and background checks, including what to expect and how to prepare for these critical stages in the application process.

Interviews and Background Checks

Successfully navigating the interviews and background checks is a critical step in the citizenship application process. These steps are designed to verify your eligibility, ensure the authenticity of your application, and assess your integration into the host country. Here's what to expect and how to prepare.

What to Expect

1. Background Checks:

- **Criminal Record Check**: Authorities will thoroughly review your criminal history. This involves checking police records from your home country and other countries where you reside.

- **Financial Due Diligence**: Your financial history will be scrutinized to ensure that your funds are legitimate and that you do not have a history of financial crimes such as money laundering or tax evasion.

- **Verification of Documents**: All submitted documents will be verified for authenticity. This includes birth certificates, marriage certificates, financial statements, and other supporting documents.

2. **Interviews**:

- **Purpose**: Interviews are conducted to assess your commitment to the host country, verify the information provided in your application, and evaluate your integration into the local community.

- **Format**: Interviews can be conducted in person, over the phone, or via videoconferencing. They may involve one or more immigration officials.

- **Content**: You will be asked about your background, reasons for seeking citizenship, understanding of the host country's culture and laws, and future plans.

Common Interview Questions:

- ❖ *Personal Background*: Questions about your personal history, family, and previous residences.
- ❖ *Motivation*: Why did you choose to apply for citizenship in this country, and how do you plan to contribute to the community?

❖ *Cultural Integration*: Your knowledge of the country's history, culture, and language and how you have integrated into the society.

❖ *Investment Details*: Specific questions about your investment, business plans, or job creation efforts.

How to Prepare

1. Gather Information:

- **Review Your Application**: Go through your application thoroughly to ensure you are familiar with all the details you provided. Be prepared to discuss any aspect of your application.

- **Understand the Country**: Research the host country's history, culture, political system, and current events. This knowledge will demonstrate your commitment to integrating into the society.

2. **Prepare Documents**:

- **Organize Originals and Copies**: Have all original documents and certified copies readily available for verification during the interview.

- **Translation**: If necessary, ensure that all documents are translated into the host country's official language.

3. **Practice Interview Skills**:

- **Mock Interviews**: Conduct mock interviews with friends, family, or a professional coach to practice answering potential questions confidently and accurately.

- **Language Proficiency**: If the interview is conducted in a language other than your native tongue, practice speaking and understanding that language to ensure clear communication.

4. **Address Potential Issues**:

- **Clarify Inconsistencies**: Be prepared to explain any discrepancies or gaps in your application. Honesty and clarity are crucial.

- **Explain Financial Transactions**: If there are large or unusual financial transactions in your history, be ready to provide explanations and documentation.

5. **Present Yourself Professionally:**

- **Dress Appropriately**: Dress in professional or business attire for the interview to make a good impression.

- **Be Punctual**: Arrive on time or log in early if the interview is conducted online.

6. **Maintain a Positive Attitude:**

- **Stay Calm and Polite**: Approach the interview calmly and respectfully. Answer questions thoughtfully and honestly.

- **Show Enthusiasm**: Demonstrate your enthusiasm for becoming a citizen and your commitment to contributing positively to the host country.

Successfully completing the interviews and background checks is a critical step toward acquiring second citizenship. By understanding what to expect and preparing thoroughly, you can confidently navigate this process. The following section will explore the final steps to citizenship, including approval and taking the oath of allegiance.

Approval and Oath

Final Steps to Citizenship

After successfully navigating the application process, including gathering necessary documents, filling out forms, and completing interviews and background checks, you will move on to the final steps toward acquiring your new citizenship. This stage involves receiving approval from the relevant authorities and participating in an oath-taking ceremony.

1. **Approval Notification**:

- **Notification of Decision**: Once your application has been thoroughly reviewed and approved, you will receive an official notification from the immigration authorities or the relevant government department.

- **Approval Letter**: This letter will outline the next steps, including any final administrative requirements and details about the oath ceremony.

2. Final Administrative Steps:

- **Fees**: Ensure that all required fees have been paid. This may include any outstanding application or processing fees.

- **Additional Documents**: You may need to submit additional documents or complete final forms. Follow the instructions provided in the approval letter carefully.

- **Residency Confirmation**: Some countries may require a final residency confirmation or a visit to the country before the oath ceremony.

Taking the Oath and Receiving Your Passport

1. The Oath Ceremony:

- **Invitation**: You will receive an invitation to an oath ceremony, a formal event in which new citizens pledge their allegiance to their new country.

- **Date and Venue**: The invitation will include the ceremony's date, time, and location. Ensure you arrive early and are prepared for the event.

- **Dress Code**: Dress in formal or business attire to show respect for the occasion.

2. The Oath of Allegiance:

- **Swearing In**: During the ceremony, you will take the oath of allegiance. It is is a solemn pledge to uphold the laws and values of your new country and to fulfill your duties as a citizen.

- **Oath Content**: The exact wording of the oath varies by country but generally includes a commitment to loyalty, obedience to the laws, and support for the country's constitution and institutions.

- **Signing the Oath**: After reciting the oath, you may be required to sign a document affirming your commitment.

3. Receiving Your Certificate of Naturalization:

- **Certificate Presentation**: Upon taking the oath, you will receive a naturalization certificate. This document officially confirms your status as a citizen.

- **Verification**: Verify all details on the certificate for accuracy. This document will be essential for obtaining your new passport and other official identification.

4. Applying for Your Passport:

  - **Passport Application**: With your certificate of naturalization in hand, you can now apply for a passport. Follow the standard passport application procedures of your new country.

  - **Required Documents**: Submit your naturalization certificate, photos, application form, and any required fees. You may also need to provide additional identification documents.

  - **Processing Time**: Passport processing times vary, so apply immediately. Some countries offer expedited processing for new citizens.

5. Enjoying Your New Citizenship:

  - **Rights and Privileges**: As a new citizen, you now have the rights and privileges of citizenship, including the ability to vote, access public services, and travel with your new passport.

  - **Responsibilities**: In addition to the benefits, you have responsibilities, such as obeying the laws, paying taxes, and participating in civic duties.

Tips for a Smooth Transition:

- ✓ *Stay Informed*: Keep abreast of any additional steps or requirements you must complete after obtaining citizenship.
- ✓ *Join Community Groups*: Consider joining community groups or associations for new citizens to help integrate into your new country
- ✓ *Maintain Dual Citizenship Requirements*: If you retain your original citizenship, ensure you understand and comply with the requirements of both countries.

By successfully completing the approval and oath-taking process, you will fully transition into your new role as a citizen of your chosen country. Congratulations on reaching this significant milestone!

In the next chapter, we will explore managing multiple passports, including legal obligations, practical considerations for travel, and how to handle cultural integration in your new country.

Managing Multiple Passports

Legal Obligations

Managing multiple passports can provide significant benefits, but it also comes with important legal obligations. Understanding and complying with these obligations is crucial to avoid legal issues and fully enjoy your Multiple Citizenships' benefits. Here's a detailed look at the key legal obligations, including reporting and tax obligations and military service considerations.

Reporting and Tax Obligations

1. **Reporting Obligations**:

Dual Citizenship Reporting: Some countries require you to report the acquisition of a second citizenship. Ensure you understand the reporting requirements of both your original and new countries of citizenship.

Travel Documentation: Always travel with the appropriate passport and ensure you enter and exit countries using the correct documentation. This helps maintain accurate records and avoid issues at border controls.

2. **Tax Obligations**:

Global Income Reporting: Many countries, such as the United States, require citizens to report global income, regardless of where it is earned. Familiarize yourself with the tax laws of all your countries of citizenship.

Double Taxation Agreements (DTAs): Some countries have DTAs that prevent double taxation on the same income. Understand how these agreements apply to you and take advantage of tax credits or exemptions.

Foreign Bank Account Reporting: You may need to report foreign bank accounts and assets. For example, U.S. citizens must file the Foreign Bank Account Report (FBAR) if their foreign account balances exceed certain thresholds.

Residency-Based Taxation: Some countries tax based on residency rather than citizenship. Ensure you understand your residency status and how it affects your tax obligations.

Tips for Managing Tax Obligations:

- ❖ Consult Tax Professionals: Work with tax advisors knowledgeable about international tax laws and the specific requirements of your countries of citizenship.
- ❖ Stay Organized: Keep detailed records of all income, expenses, and financial transactions. This will help you accurately report your taxes and take advantage of any available deductions or credits.
- ❖ Plan Ahead: Consider the tax implications of financial decisions, such as investments and property purchases, in all countries where you hold citizenship.

Military Service Considerations

1. Mandatory Military Service:

Dual Citizenship and Military Obligations: Some countries have mandatory military service requirements. As a dual citizen, you may be obligated to serve in the military of one or both countries of citizenship.

Service Exemptions and Deferrals: Check if exemptions or deferrals are available. Some countries offer exemptions for individuals who reside abroad or have already served in another country's military.

2. **Conflict of Interest**:

Avoiding Conflicts Serving in one country's military could potentially create conflicts of interest or legal issues in another country. Understand the policies and potential consequences before making decisions about military service.

Communication with Authorities: If you face conflicting military obligations, communicate with the relevant authorities in both countries to understand your options and obligations. Seek legal advice if necessary.

3. **Documentation and Proof:**

Maintain Records: Keep detailed records of military service, exemptions, or deferrals. This documentation can be crucial if you need to prove your compliance with military obligations in the future.

Legal Advice: Consult with legal experts specializing in military service laws for dual citizens to ensure you fully comply with all requirements.

Tips for Managing Military Service Obligations:

➢ Stay Informed: Regularly check for updates or changes to military service laws in your countries of citizenship.

➢ Plan Proactively: If you know you may be subject to military service obligations, plan your residence and travel accordingly to minimize disruptions.

➢ Seek Legal Assistance: When in doubt, seek legal assistance to navigate complex military service requirements and avoid potential legal issues.

Understanding and managing the legal obligations associated with multiple passports is essential for maintaining compliance and enjoying the benefits of your dual or Multiple Citizenships. In the next section, we will explore practical considerations for travel, including how to use your multiple passports effectively and manage renewals and replacements.

Practical Considerations

Traveling with Multiple Passports

Traveling with multiple passports can offer significant advantages, such as increased travel flexibility and access to more countries. However, it also requires careful management to ensure a smooth and hassle-free experience. Here are some practical tips for traveling with multiple passports:

1. **Entry and Exit Procedures**:

Use the Correct Passport: When entering and exiting a country, always use the passport that offers the most favorable terms for that particular country. For example, if one of your passports allows visa-free entry, use that passport.

Consistency: Ensure you consistently use the same passport for entry and exit in a particular country to avoid confusion and potential issues with immigration authorities.

2. Border Control and Customs:

Declare Dual Citizenship: Be prepared to declare your dual citizenship status if asked by border control officers. Carry both passports and any additional documentation that might be required.

Customs Declarations: Follow each country's customs regulations, declaring any items or currency as required by law.

3. Visa and Travel Requirements:

Check Visa Requirements: Before traveling, check the visa requirements for each country using the specific passport you intend to use. Some countries have different visa requirements for different nationalities.

Apply for Visas in Advance: If a visa is required, apply well in advance to avoid delays. Make sure you know which passport to submit for the visa application.

4. Managing Multiple Passports:

Keep Passports Separate: Keep your passports in separate, secure locations to avoid losing both simultaneously. This can help prevent travel disruptions if one passport is lost or stolen.

Digital Copies: Make digital copies of your passports and store them securely online. This can be useful for reference and in case of emergencies.

Tips for Smooth Travel:

- ➤ Research Travel Policies: Understand the entry and exit policies of each country you plan to visit, including any special considerations for dual citizens.
- ➤ Stay Organized: Keep a travel folder with all necessary documents, including visas, itineraries, and copies of your passports.
- ➤ Be Prepared for Questions: Immigration officers may ask about your dual citizenship status. Answer honestly and confidently, providing any necessary documentation.

Renewals and Replacements

Managing the renewal and replacement of multiple passports is crucial to ensure uninterrupted travel and legal compliance. Here are the critical considerations for renewing and replacing your passports:

1. **Passport Renewals**:

   - **Expiration Dates**: Keep track of the expiration dates of all your passports. Most countries require passports to be valid for at least six months beyond your travel dates.

   - **Renewal Procedures**: Each country has its renewal procedures, which may include submitting a renewal application, providing updated photos, and paying a fee.

   - **Processing Times**: Renewal processing times can vary. Apply for renewals well in advance to avoid being without a valid passport during travel.

2. **Passport Replacements**:

   - **Lost or Stolen Passports**: If a passport is lost or stolen, report it immediately to the relevant authorities of the issuing country and obtain a police report if required.

- **Emergency Passports**: Some countries offer emergency passports or temporary travel documents for urgent travel needs. Check with your country's embassy or consulate for assistance.

- **Replacement Procedures**: Follow the replacement procedures outlined by the issuing country. These may involve submitting a new application, providing identification, and paying a fee.

Tips for Managing Renewals and Replacements:

➤ Set Reminders: Use digital calendars or apps to set reminders for passport expiration dates and renewal deadlines.

➤ Keep Copies: Maintain copies of all important pages of your passports, including personal information and visa pages, to assist in the replacement process if needed.

➤ Stay Informed: Regularly check the passport renewal and replacement policies of your country of citizenship, as these can change over time.

By understanding the practical considerations of traveling with multiple passports and effectively managing renewals and replacements, you can enjoy the benefits of your Multiple Citizenships without disruptions. The next section will explore cultural integration, including living in a new country, building a network, and fostering a sense of community.

Cultural Integration

Successfully integrating into a new culture is vital to managing Multiple Citizenships. It involves adapting to new social norms, understanding local customs, and building meaningful connections within the community. Here's a guide to navigating cultural integration effectively.

Living in a New Country

1. **Understanding Local Customs and Traditions**:
   - ➤ Research and Learn: Before moving, research your new country's local customs, traditions, and social norms. Understanding these cultural nuances can help you avoid misunderstandings and show respect for your new community.

> Participate in Local Events: Engage in local festivals, holidays, and community events to immerse yourself in the culture. This participation can help you connect with locals and understand the cultural significance of various traditions.

2. **Language Proficiency**:

> Learn the Language: If the primary language of your new country is different from your native tongue, invest time in learning it. Language classes, online courses, and language exchange programs can be valuable resources.

> Practice Regularly: Use the language in daily interactions, such as shopping, dining, and socializing. Practice helps improve fluency and boosts confidence in using the language.

3. **Adapt to Social Norms**:

> Observe and Adapt: Pay attention to how locals interact in social settings, including greetings, body language, and etiquette. Adapting to these norms demonstrates respect and facilitates smoother social interactions.

➤ Respect Local Laws: Familiarize yourself with local laws and regulations to ensure compliance and avoid legal issues.

4. Managing Daily Life:

➤ Housing and Utilities: Understand the process of renting or buying a home, setting up utilities, and managing household services in your new country.

➤ Healthcare: Learn about the local healthcare system, including accessing medical services, finding a doctor, and obtaining health insurance.

➤ Education: If you have children, research the local education system and explore schooling options, including public, private, and international schools.

Building a Network and Community

1. Social Connections:

➤ Join Expat Communities: Connect with expatriate communities through social media groups, local meetups, and expat organizations. These communities can provide valuable support, advice, and social opportunities.

➤ Engage with Locals: Make an effort to build relationships with residents. Attend community events, volunteer, and participate in local clubs or sports teams to meet people and establish connections.

2. **Professional Networking**:

➤ Attend Networking Events: Join professional associations and attend industry events, conferences, and networking sessions to build your professional network in your new country.

➤ Leverage Online Platforms: Use platforms like LinkedIn to connect with professionals in your field and join industry-specific groups and forums.

3. **Community Involvement**:

➤ Volunteer: Volunteering for local causes and organizations is a great way to give back to the community and meet like-minded individuals.

➤ Join Clubs and Groups: Participate in clubs, hobby groups, and social organizations that align with your interests, such as sports, arts, or cultural groups.

4. **Family Integration**:

➤ Involve Your Family: Ensure that your family members, including children and spouses, are also integrating well. Enroll children in schools and extracurricular activities and encourage family participation in community events.

➤ Cultural Exchange: Share your cultural traditions with your new community while embracing and respecting theirs. This exchange can enrich your experience and foster mutual understanding.

Tips for Successful Cultural Integration:

➤ Be Open-Minded: Approach your new environment with an open mind and a willingness to learn and adapt.

➤ Seek Support: If you encounter challenges, don't hesitate to seek support from local organizations, expat groups, or professional services.

➢ Be Patient: Cultural integration is a gradual process that takes time. Be patient with yourself and others as you navigate this transition.

➢ Embrace Differences: Celebrate the differences you encounter and view them as opportunities for growth and enrichment.

By actively engaging in cultural integration, you can build a fulfilling and enriching life in your new country, making the most of the opportunities Multiple Citizenships provide. In the next chapter, we will explore real-life examples of individuals who have successfully navigated the path to Multiple Citizenships, sharing their stories and insights.

Case Studies and Success Stories

Real-Life Examples

Learning from the experiences of others can provide valuable insights and inspiration for your journey towards Multiple Citizenships. In this chapter, we will explore the personal stories of individuals who have successfully acquired Multiple Citizenships, highlighting the lessons they learned and best practices they adopted along the way. Names and specific details have been changed for privacy reasons.

Personal Stories of Successful Multiple Citizenships

Sarah's Journey to Dual Citizenship in Canada and Portugal

Background:

Sarah, a successful entrepreneur from Canada, decided to pursue Portuguese citizenship to expand her business opportunities in Europe and enjoy the lifestyle benefits of living in a warmer climate.

The Process:

- **Research and Planning**: Sarah began by thoroughly researching Portugal's Golden Visa program. She then consulted with immigration lawyers to understand the requirements and implications.

- **Investment in Real Estate**: She decided to invest €500,000 in a property in Lisbon, which qualified her for the Golden Visa.

- **Residency and Integration**: Sarah spent the required time in Portugal each year, learning Portuguese and integrating into the local community.

- **Naturalization**: Sarah applied for Portuguese citizenship after six years of residency. Her application was approved, and she became a dual citizen of Canada and Portugal.

Lessons Learned:

- ✓ Professional Advice: Consulting with professionals helped Sarah navigate the legal and financial complexities of the process.
- ✓ Cultural Integration: Actively participating in the local community and learning the language were crucial for a smooth transition.
- ✓ Patience and Persistence: The process took several years, requiring patience and consistent effort.

Best Practices:

- ✓ Thorough Research: Understand all the requirements and implications before starting the process.
- ✓ Engage Local Experts: Work with local legal and financial advisors to ensure compliance with all regulations.

- ✓ Plan for Long-Term: Be prepared for a multi-year commitment and plan accordingly.

John's Path to Triple Citizenship in the USA, Ireland, and Italy

Background:

John, a software engineer from the USA, leveraged his ancestral connections to obtain Irish and Italian citizenship. This move provided him with greater flexibility for travel and work across Europe.

The Process:

Citizenship by Descent in Ireland: John discovered that he was eligible for Irish citizenship through his grandmother, who was born in Ireland. He gathered the necessary documents, including birth and marriage certificates, and applied for citizenship.

Citizenship by Descent in Italy: John also qualified for Italian citizenship through his great-grandfather. This process required extensive documentation and verification, but he eventually succeeded.

Balancing Multiple Obligations: John carefully managed the legal obligations of holding Multiple Citizenships, including tax and reporting requirements.

Lessons Learned:

- ✓ Documentation is Key: Gathering and verifying ancestral documents can be challenging, but they are essential for citizenship by descent.
- ✓ Understanding Legal Obligations: It is crucial to be aware of and comply with each country's legal obligations.
- ✓ Flexibility and Adaptability: Balancing Multiple Citizenships requires flexibility and adaptation to different legal and cultural environments.

Best Practices:

- ✓ Detailed Documentation: Maintain thorough records of all necessary documents and ensure they are certified and translated if needed.
- ✓ Stay Informed: Keep up-to-date with each citizenship's legal requirements and obligations.

✓ Plan for Travel: Use the most appropriate passport for each travel situation to maximize benefits and avoid complications.

Lessons Learned and Best Practices

1. Thorough Research and Preparation:

- **Understand Requirements**: Before starting the application process, ensure you understand each country's specific requirements and timelines.

- **Seek Professional Help**: Engaging immigration lawyers, financial advisors, and local experts can provide invaluable assistance and ensure compliance with all regulations.

2. Financial Planning:

- **Budget for Costs**: Citizenship applications, investments, and legal fees can be significant. Plan your budget carefully to cover all associated costs.

- **Consider Tax Implications**: Understand each country's tax obligations and benefits to optimize your financial planning.

3. Cultural Integration:

- **Learn the Language**: Learning the local language can significantly enhance your integration and help you build connections within the community.

- **Participate in Local Life**: Engage in local customs, traditions, and community activities to foster a sense of belonging and acceptance.

4. Patience and Persistence:

- **Expect Delays**: The citizenship application process can be lengthy and may involve unexpected delays. Be patient and persistent in your efforts.

- **Stay Organized**: Keep all documents, correspondence, and records organized and easily accessible.

5. Flexibility and Adaptability:

- **Be Prepared for Change**: Legal and regulatory changes can impact your citizenship status and obligations. Stay informed and be prepared to adapt as needed.

- **Manage Multiple Obligations**: Understand and comply with each country's legal, tax, and residency obligations to avoid complications.

These real-life examples and lessons learned can provide valuable insights and inspiration for your own journey towards Multiple Citizenships. In the next chapter, we will address frequently asked questions, offering straightforward answers and practical advice for common concerns and misconceptions about acquiring and managing Multiple Citizenships.

Expert Insights

Gaining perspectives from professionals who specialize in immigration law and consultancy can provide invaluable insights into the process of acquiring and managing Multiple Citizenships. This section features interviews with immigration lawyers and consultants who share their expertise, tips, and experiences.

Interviews with Immigration Lawyers and Consultants

Interview 1: Maria Sanchez, Immigration Lawyer

Background:

Maria Sanchez is an experienced immigration lawyer based in Madrid, Spain. She specializes in citizenship and residency through investment programs and has helped numerous clients successfully acquire second and third passports.

Q: What are the most common mistakes applicants make when applying for citizenship by investment?

Maria:

One of the most common mistakes is not thoroughly researching the target country's program requirements and legal obligations. Applicants often need to pay more attention to details such as the specific documentation required, the timeline for the investment, and the residency requirements. Another mistake is attempting to handle the entire process without professional help. Immigration laws are complex, and having an experienced lawyer can make a significant difference in ensuring a smooth application process.

Q: What advice would you give to someone considering applying for a second citizenship?

Maria:

Firstly, do your homework. Understand the benefits and obligations of the citizenship program you are interested in. Secondly, consult with an immigration lawyer early in the process. They can guide the best investment options, help gather the necessary documentation, and navigate legal hurdles. Finally, be patient and persistent. The process can take time, but with proper planning and support, it can be a rewarding endeavor.

Interview 2: James Taylor, Immigration Consultant

Background:

James Taylor is an immigration consultant based in London, UK. He has over 15 years of experience assisting clients with obtaining citizenship through various investment and residency programs worldwide.

Q: How do you help clients choose the best citizenship-by-investment program for their needs?

James:

Choosing the right program depends on the client's goals, financial situation, and personal circumstances. I start by understanding the client's priorities, such as visa-free travel, tax benefits, or quality of life. I then present them with options that align with their goals and provide a detailed analysis of each program's requirements and benefits. We also discuss potential challenges and how to overcome them. My role is to ensure clients make informed decisions that best suit their needs.

Q: What trends are you seeing in the citizenship by investment market?

James:

One notable trend is the increasing interest in European programs, notably those offering residency that leads to citizenship, like Portugal's Golden Visa. Clients are attracted to EU citizenship's stability, quality of life, and travel benefits. There's growing interest in Caribbean programs due to their relatively low investment thresholds and quick processing times. Another trend is the rising importance of dual citizenship for business and financial planning, as it offers greater flexibility and security.

Interview 3: Amina Khan, Immigration Lawyer and Consultant

Background:

Amina Khan is an immigration lawyer and consultant based in Dubai, UAE. She specializes in helping high-net-worth individuals and families obtain second citizenships through investment programs.

Q: What are the key factors to consider when preparing an application for citizenship by investment?

Amina:

The key factors include ensuring that all documentation is accurate, up-to-date, and certified. It's also essential to understand the financial requirements and ensure that the source of funds is transparent and well-documented. Additionally, applicants should be aware of the legal obligations of new citizenship, such as tax liabilities and residency requirements. Preparing a thorough and well-organized application can significantly increase the chances of success.

Q: How do you handle complex cases, such as those involving multiple family members or complicated financial histories?

Amina:

Complex cases require a meticulous approach and attention to detail. For multiple family members, it's essential to gather all necessary documentation for each individual and ensure that each application component aligns with the family's overall goals. I work closely with financial advisors to present a clear and transparent financial narrative for complicated financial histories. This may involve detailed explanations and additional documentation to satisfy the due diligence requirements of the host country. Clear communication and comprehensive planning are essential in these cases.

Expert Tips and Best Practices:

1. **Thorough Preparation:**

 - Ensure that all required documents are complete, certified, and translated if necessary.

 - Double-check all information for accuracy and consistency across all forms and documents.

2. **Professional Guidance:**

 - Engage with experienced immigration lawyers and consultants who can provide expert advice and navigate the complexities of the application process.

 - Utilize their knowledge to avoid common pitfalls and ensure compliance with all legal requirements.

3. **Clear Financial Documentation**:

 - Provide transparent and well-documented financial information to meet the investment and due diligence requirements.

 - Work with financial advisors to prepare clear explanations of the source of funds and investment plans.

4. **Patience and Persistence**:

 - Be prepared for a potentially lengthy process and remain patient.

 - Follow up regularly with immigration authorities and your legal team to track the progress of your application.

5. **Integration and Adaptation**:

 - Engage with the local community and try to integrate culturally and socially.

 - Learn the language and participate in local events to demonstrate commitment to your new country.

These expert insights provide valuable guidance and practical advice for anyone considering the journey toward

Multiple Citizenships. By learning from experienced professionals, you can navigate the process more effectively and achieve your goals more confidently.

In the next chapter, we will address frequently asked questions, offering clear answers and practical advice for common concerns and misconceptions about acquiring and managing Multiple Citizenships.

Frequently Asked Questions

Common Concerns and Misconceptions

Navigating the process of acquiring Multiple Citizenships can be complex, and it's expected to have questions and concerns. This chapter addresses some typical queries and clarifies common myths to help you better understand the realities of Multiple Citizenships.

Addressing Typical Queries

Q: Is it legal to have Multiple Citizenships?

A: Yes, it is legal to have Multiple Citizenships, but it depends on the laws of the countries involved. Some countries fully recognize dual or Multiple Citizenships, while others may have restrictions or require you to renounce your original citizenship. Always check the specific regulations of each country.

Q: How long does it take to acquire a second citizenship?

A:* The timeline for acquiring a second citizenship varies widely depending on the method and the country. Citizenship by investment programs can take as little as a few months, while naturalization processes based on residency can take several years. Research the specific program you are interested in for accurate timelines.

Q: Do I have to live in the country where I am applying for citizenship?

A: Residency requirements vary by program. Some citizenship by investment programs have minimal or no residency requirements, while others may require you to live in the country for a certain period. It's essential to understand and comply with these requirements to maintain eligibility.

Q: Will having Multiple Citizenships affect my tax obligations?

A: Having Multiple Citizenships can affect your tax obligations. Some countries tax based on citizenship, while others tax based on residency. You may need to file tax returns in multiple countries and could be subject to double taxation, although tax treaties often help mitigate this. Consult with a tax advisor to understand your specific situation.

Q: Can my family members also obtain citizenship?

A: Many citizenship programs allow family members, including spouses and dependent children, to be included in the application. Some programs also extend benefits to parents or grandparents. Check the specific eligibility criteria for family members in the program you are applying for.

Q: What happens if my application is denied?

A: If your application is denied, you can usually appeal the decision or reapply after addressing the reasons for denial. Understanding the grounds for denial and seeking professional advice to improve your chances in subsequent applications is essential.

Clarifying Myths

Myth 1: Multiple Citizenships are only for the wealthy.

Reality: While some citizenship-by-investment programs require substantial financial investments, other pathways, such as citizenship by descent or naturalization through residency, are accessible to a broader range of individuals. Each pathway has different costs and requirements.

Myth 2: Dual citizens have to pay taxes in both countries.

Reality: Dual citizens may have tax obligations in both countries, but double taxation treaties often exist to prevent paying taxes twice on the same income. Consulting with a tax professional can help you navigate and optimize your tax situation.

Myth 3: You must renounce your original citizenship to acquire a new one.

Reality: This depends on the countries involved. Some countries require renunciation, while others allow dual or Multiple Citizenships. It's essential to check the laws of both your original country and the country where you seek new citizenship.

Myth 4: Having multiple passports makes international travel complicated.

Reality: While traveling with multiple passports requires careful management, it can also offer significant benefits, such as increased travel flexibility and access to more visa-free destinations. Staying organized and informed about entry and exit requirements for each passport can simplify travel.

Myth 5: Citizenship by investment is a guaranteed and quick process.

Reality: While some citizenship-by-investment programs offer expedited processing, there are no guarantees. Each application undergoes thorough due diligence, and various factors can delay the process. It's important to have realistic expectations and prepare accordingly.

Myth 6: You can lose your original citizenship if you acquire a new one.

Reality: Whether you lose your original citizenship upon acquiring a new one depends on the laws of your original country. Some countries automatically revoke citizenship if you acquire another, while others allow dual citizenship. Always verify with the relevant authorities.

Tips for Addressing Concerns and Misconceptions:

- ✓ Research Thoroughly: Ensure you understand each citizenship program's specific requirements, benefits, and obligations.
- ✓ Consult Professionals: Seek advice from immigration lawyers, tax advisors, and other professionals to clarify doubts and navigate complex situations.
- ✓ Stay Informed: Keep up-to-date with changes in immigration laws and policies that might affect your citizenship status or application process.

By addressing common concerns and clarifying misconceptions, you can make informed decisions and more effectively navigate the process of acquiring and managing Multiple Citizenships.

In the next chapter, we will explore resources and further reading. We will provide helpful websites, organizations, books, and articles to deepen your understanding and assist you in your journey toward Multiple Citizenships.

Resources and Further Reading

Useful Websites and Organizations

Navigating acquiring and managing Multiple Citizenships can be complex, but numerous resources are available. This chapter lists valuable websites and organizations, including immigration services and government portals, to help you gather information, stay updated, and find professional assistance.

Global Citizen Life

- **Website** https://www.GlobalCitizenLife.org

- **Description**: A boutique consulting firm specializes in helping clients legally minimize their taxes, secure citizenships and residencies, protect assets, and manage international investments. Their work enables individuals to thrive in diverse economic landscapes, free from the confines of any single government's control.

International Organization for Migration (IOM)

- **Website:** www.iom.int

- **Description**: The IOM provides comprehensive information and assistance on migration issues, including citizenship and residency programs. Their resources include research, policy recommendations, and practical guides for migrants.

Immigration and Refugee Board of Canada (IRB)

- **Website:** www.irb-cisr.gc.ca

- **Description**: The IRB is Canada's largest independent administrative tribunal, responsible for making decisions on immigration and refugee matters. Their website offers resources on immigration policies, procedures, and legal support.

Government Portals

U.S. Citizenship and Immigration Services (USCIS)

- **Website:** www.uscis.gov

- **Description**: USCIS is the government agency overseeing immigration to the United States. Their website provides detailed information on visa categories, naturalization, citizenship applications, and policy updates.

Government of Canada - Immigration, Refugees and Citizenship Canada (IRCC)

- **Website**: www.canada.ca/en/immigration-refugees-citizenship.html

- **Description**: IRCC manages immigration and citizenship in Canada. Their website offers information on various immigration programs, including Express Entry, family sponsorship, citizenship applications, and application guides and forms.

European Union Immigration Portal

- **Website**: https://ec.europa.eu/immigration

- **Description**: This portal provides comprehensive information on immigration policies, rights, and procedures within the European Union. It covers visas, work permits, family reunification, and long-term residency.

Australian Government - Department of Home Affairs

- **Website**: www.homeaffairs.gov.au

- **Description:** The Department of Home Affairs oversees immigration and border protection in Australia. Their website includes visa information, citizenship, border security, and policy updates.

U.K. Government - Visas and Immigration

- **Website:** www.gov.uk/government/organisations/uk-visas-and-immigration

- **Description**: This official U.K. government portal provides detailed information on visa categories, citizenship applications, and immigration policies. It includes application forms, guidance documents, and processing times.

In the conclusion of this book, we will summarize the key points covered and provide final thoughts on embracing the journey toward Multiple Citizenships and global freedom.

Final Thoughts

Embracing Global Citizenship

Global citizenship is more relevant and attainable than ever in today's interconnected world. Having Multiple Citizenships opens doors to unparalleled opportunities, increased mobility, and enhanced personal and financial security. As we have explored throughout this book, the journey to acquiring additional passports involves careful planning, thorough research, and a deep understanding of your chosen countries' legal and cultural landscapes.

Global citizenship is not just about the practical benefits— it's about embracing a mindset that values diversity, adaptability, and a broader perspective on the world. Living the Global Citizen Lifestyle can enrich your life with new experiences, foster cross-cultural connections, and contribute positively to multiple communities.

Encouragement for Your Journey

Embarking on the journey to Multiple Citizenships can be complex and challenging but immensely rewarding. Here are some final thoughts and encouragements to guide you on your path:

1. Stay Informed and Prepared:

- Keep up-to-date with the latest information and requirements for the citizenship programs you are interested in. Staying informed will help you navigate the process more smoothly and avoid pitfalls.

2. Seek Professional Guidance:

- Don't hesitate to seek the advice of immigration lawyers, financial advisors, and other professionals specializing in citizenship through investment and residency programs. Their expertise can provide invaluable support and increase your chances of success.

3. Embrace Cultural Integration:

- Take the time to learn about and immerse yourself in the cultures of your new countries. Building strong connections and understanding local customs will enhance your experience and help you feel more at home.

4. **Plan for the Long Term:**

- Consider the long-term implications of your decisions, including tax obligations, legal responsibilities, and the impact on your family. Strategic planning will ensure you can fully enjoy the benefits of your Multiple Citizenships.

5. **Stay Positive and Persistent:**

- The path to Multiple Citizenships can be long and sometimes challenging. Stay positive, be patient, and persist through any obstacles. The rewards at the end of the journey are worthwhile.

Global Citizen Life

At Global Citizen Life, we are dedicated to helping individuals like you achieve their dreams of global citizenship. Our mission is to provide you with the tools, resources, and support to navigate the complexities of acquiring and managing Multiple Citizenships. Whether you are an entrepreneur seeking new business opportunities, a retiree looking for a new place to call home, or simply someone who values global citizenship's freedom and flexibility, we are here to guide you every step of the way.

By embracing the challenge of change and innovation, you are not just obtaining additional passports—you are building a life that transcends borders and opens up a world of possibilities. We encourage you to take bold steps, explore new horizons, and create a future where you can thrive as a global citizen.

Thank you for joining us on this journey. We wish you the best of luck in pursuing Multiple Citizenships and a fulfilling global lifestyle. Welcome to Global Citizen Life—your passport to freedom and opportunity.

Appendices

Glossary of Terms

Understanding the terminology used in citizenship and residency applications is essential. Here are some key terms you may encounter:

Dual Citizenship: Holding citizenship in two countries simultaneously.

Naturalization: The process by which a foreign national acquires citizenship of a country.

Residency by Investment (RBI): A program that grants residency status to individuals who make a significant financial investment in a country.

Citizenship by Investment (CBI): A program that grants citizenship to individuals who make a substantial investment in a country.

Visa-Free Travel: The ability to travel to certain countries without a visa.

Due Diligence: A comprehensive appraisal of an individual's background, often conducted during the citizenship application.

Permanent Residency: The right to live indefinitely in a country without becoming a citizen.

Naturalization Certificate: A document that certifies an individual has been granted citizenship through naturalization.

Oath of Allegiance: A formal declaration of loyalty to the country of new citizenship.

Tax Residency: The status of being subject to a country's tax laws, often based on residency rather than citizenship.

Checklist for Applicants

A comprehensive checklist ensures you have all the necessary documents and information before submitting your application. Here's a sample checklist for a citizenship by investment application:

Pre-Application:

[ ] Research and select the appropriate citizenship program.

[ ] Consult with an immigration lawyer or consultant.

[ ] Understand the legal and tax implications.

Personal Documents:

[ ] Certified copies of birth certificates (applicant and dependents).

[ ] Certified copies of marriage certificates (if applicable).

[ ] Copies of passports (current and previous).

Proof of Residency:

[ ] Recent utility bills or bank statements showing current address.

[ ] Copies of any residency permits held.

Financial Documents:

[ ] Bank statements (last 6-12 months).

[ ] Proof of investment (real estate purchase, business investment, etc.).

[ ] Tax returns (last 2-3 years).

Background Checks:

[ ] Police clearance certificates from all countries of residence.

[ ] Medical reports (if required).

Application Forms:

[ ] Completed citizenship application form.

[ ] Completed investment application form (if separate).

[ ] Signed declarations and affidavits.

Supporting Documents:

[ ] Proof of language proficiency (if required).

[ ] Educational certificates.

[ ] Employment history and reference letters.

Fees and Payments:

[ ] Payment of application fees.

[ ] Payment of due diligence fees.

[ ] Payment of investment amount.

Submission:

[ ] Review all forms and documents for accuracy and completeness.

[ ] Make copies of all submitted documents for your records.

[ ] Submit the application and supporting documents to the appropriate authority.

Post-Submission:

[ ] Keep track of application status and any requests for additional information.

[ ] Prepare for interviews and background checks if required.

[ ] Plan for travel and residency requirements.

By following this checklist, you can ensure that your application is thorough and complete, increasing your chances of a successful outcome.

This concludes *"Passport to Freedom: A Comprehensive Guide to Acquiring Additional Citizenships."* We hope this book has provided valuable insights and practical guidance on your journey to global citizenship. Good luck and safe travels as you embark on this exciting new chapter of your life with Global Citizen Life!